Bottlenose Dolphin

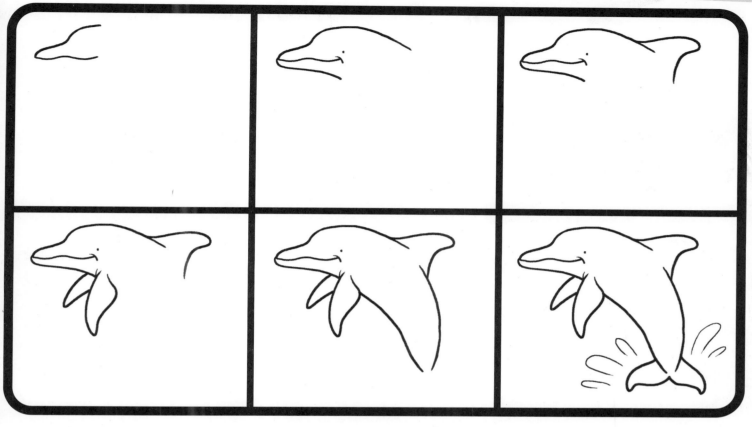

Moorish Idol

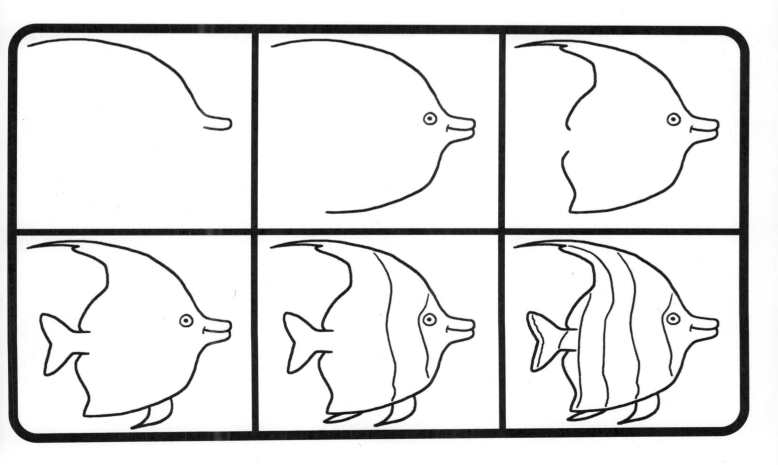

Dolphin fish

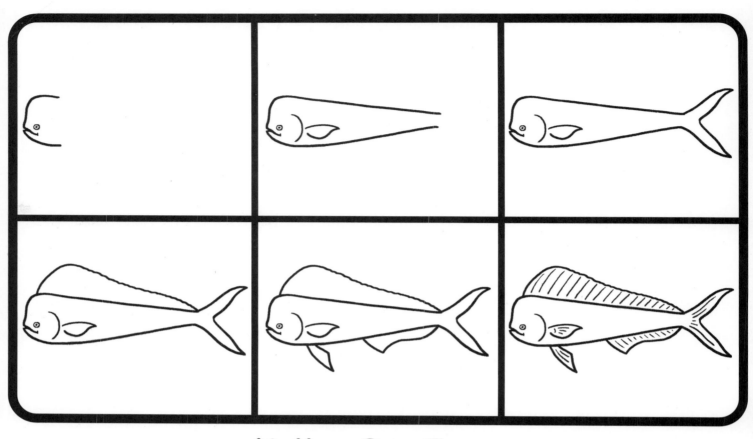

Yellowfin Tuna

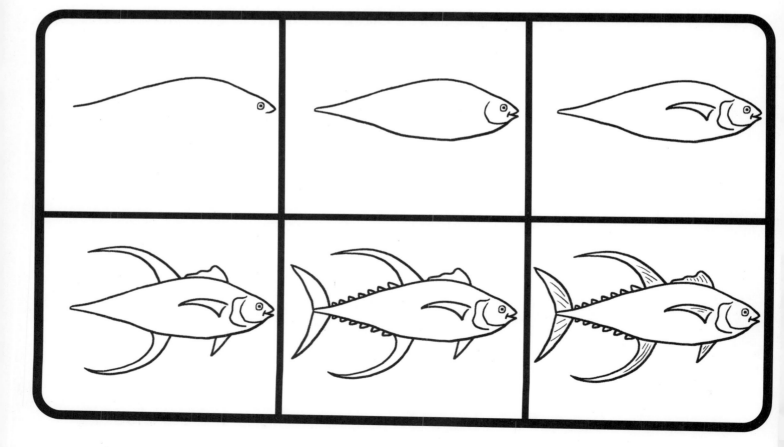

Rockhopper Penguin

Northern Right Whale

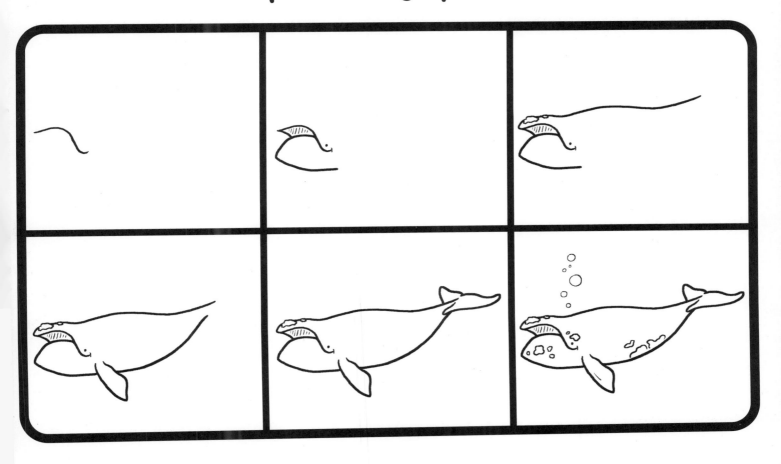

Seahorse

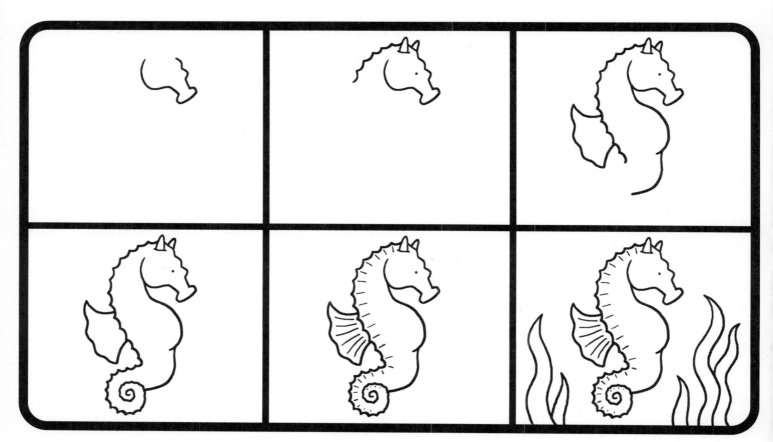

Dolphin and Calf

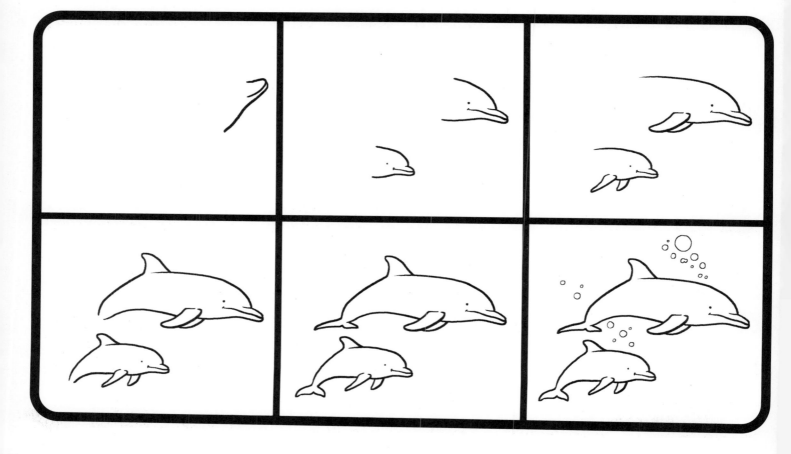

Great White Shark

Yellow Tang

Banded Pipefish

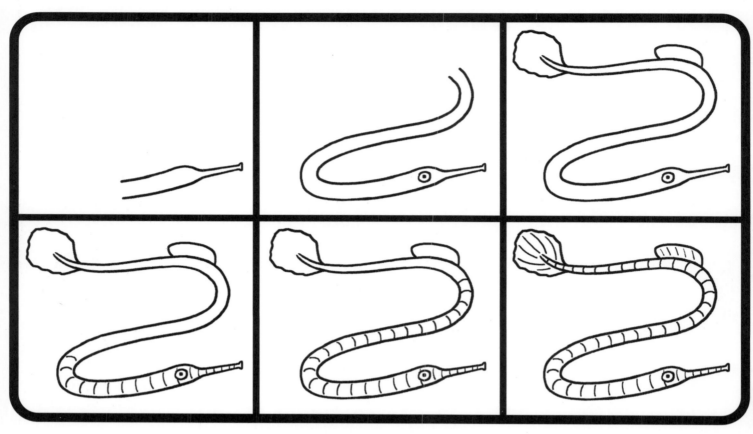

Puffer fish

Shrimp

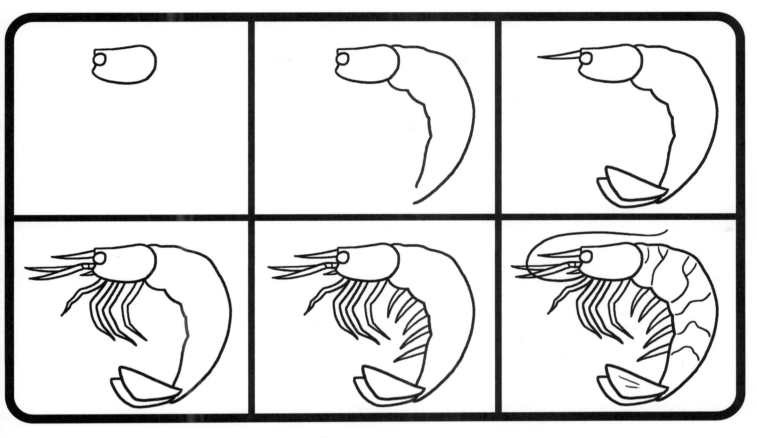

Dugong

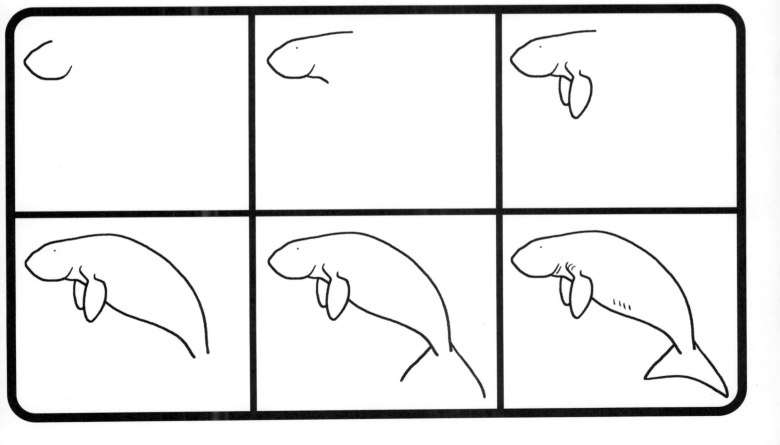

Brown Pelican

Lantern fish

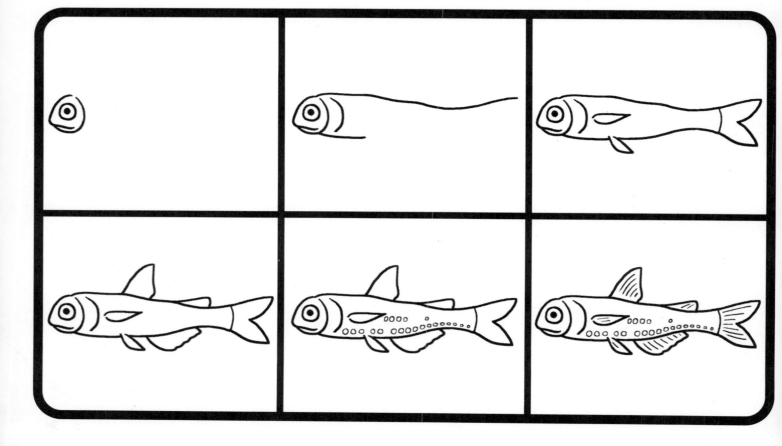

Squid

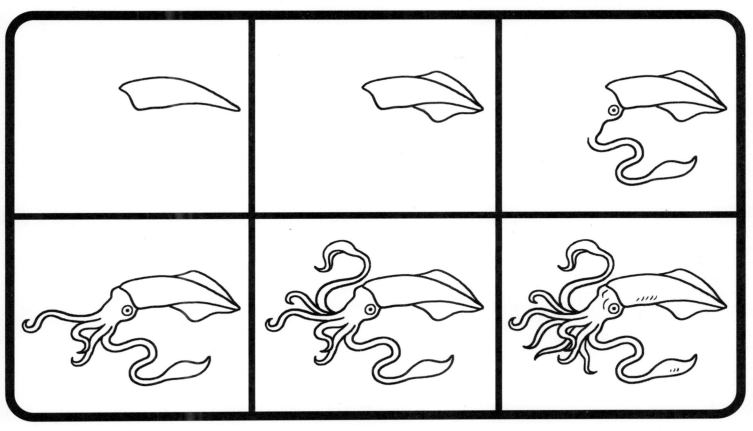

Laughing Dolphin

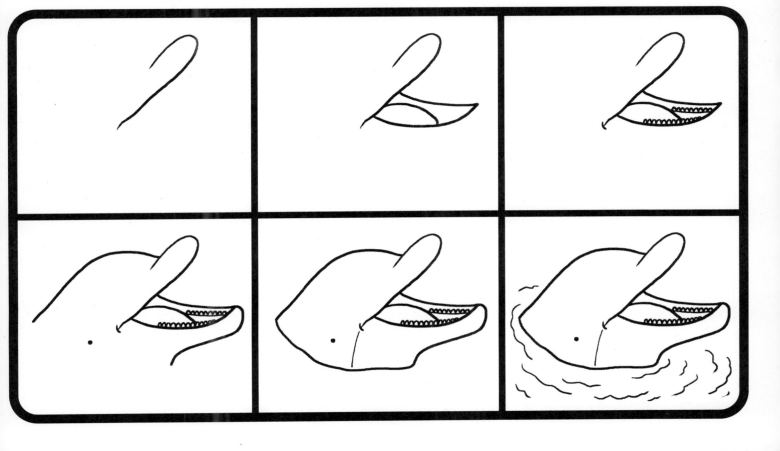

Parrot fish

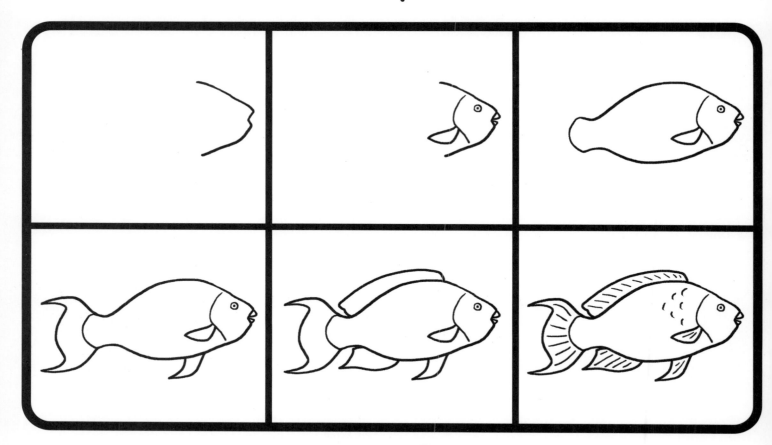

Chinstrap Penguin

Lionfish

Bonnethead Shark

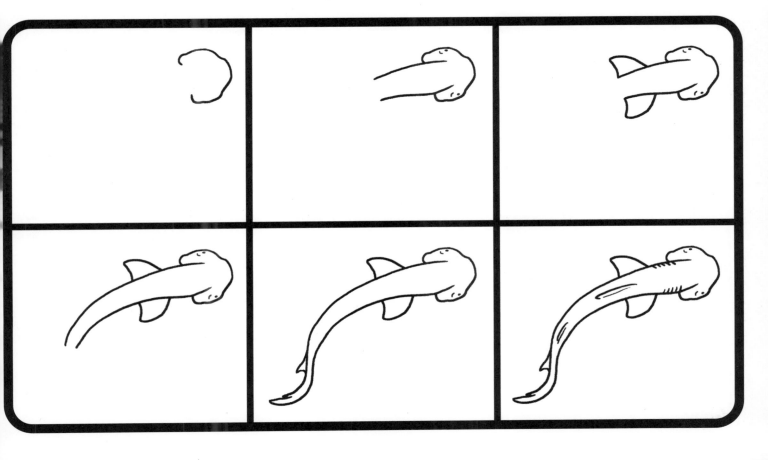

Common Dolphin

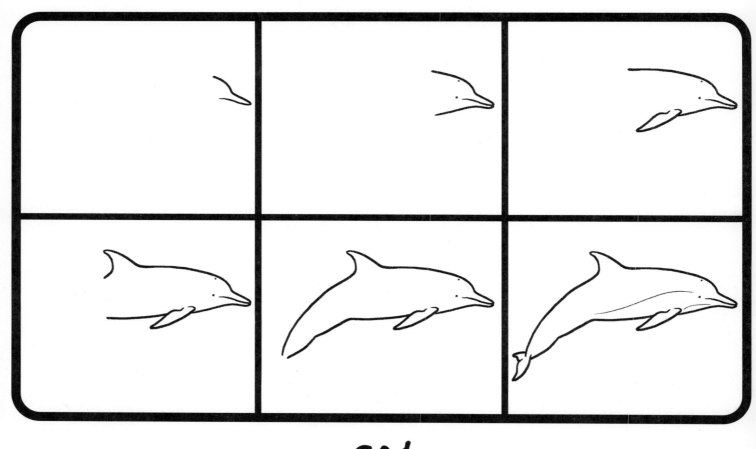

Cod

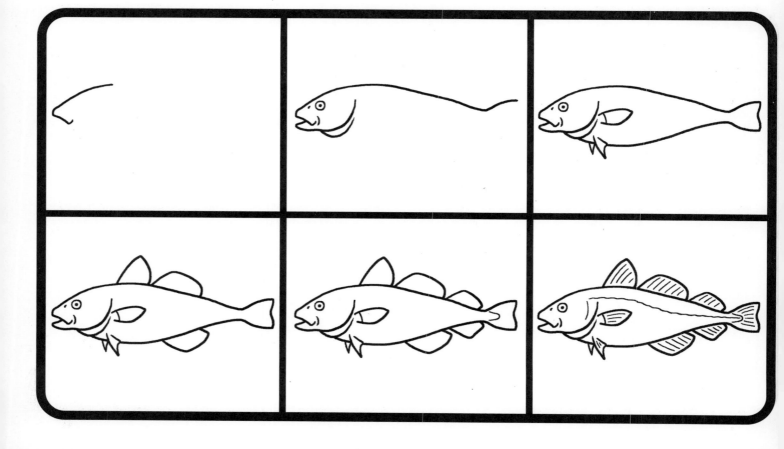

Elephant fish

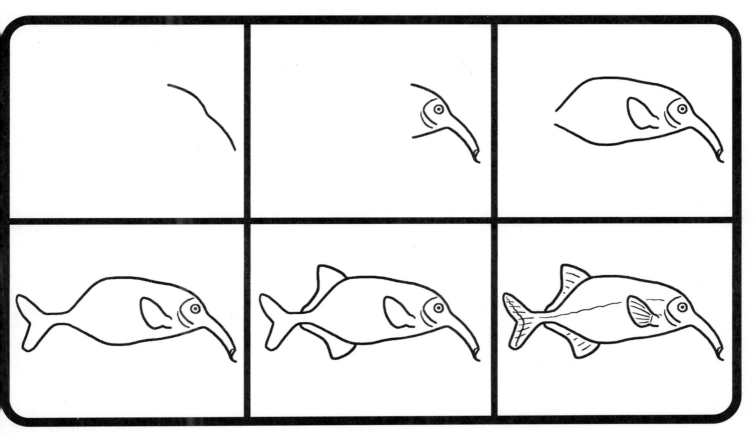

Sperm Whale

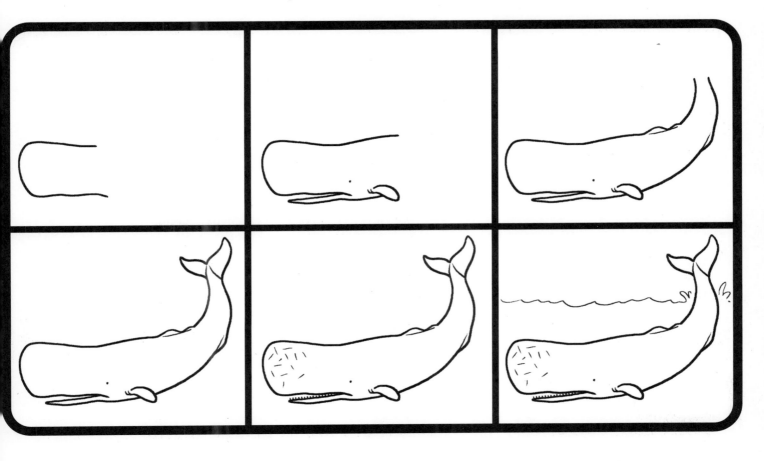

Dolphins playing

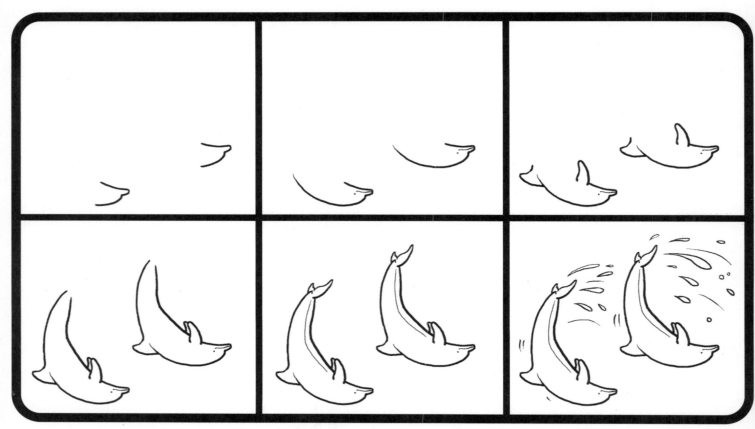

Blue Marlin

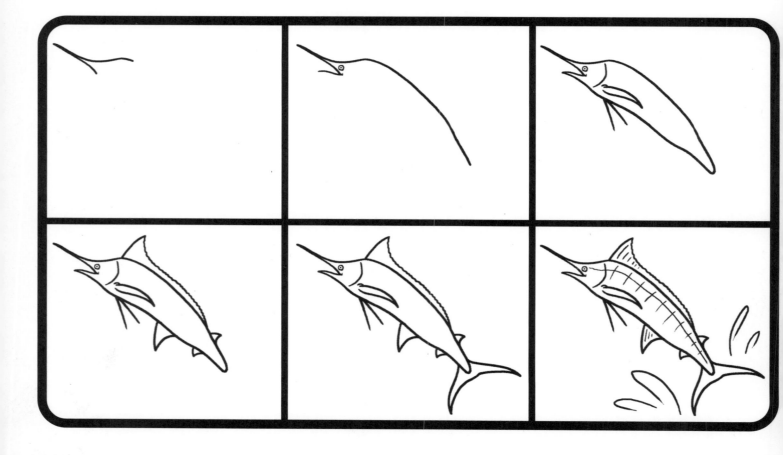

common Puffin

Lobster

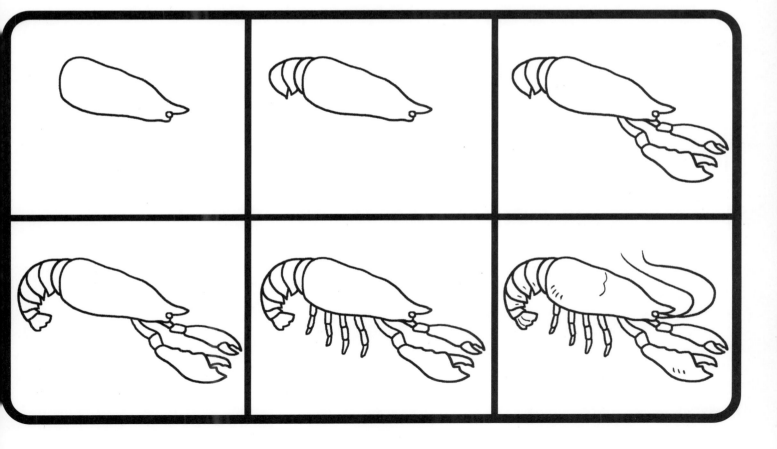

Clownfish

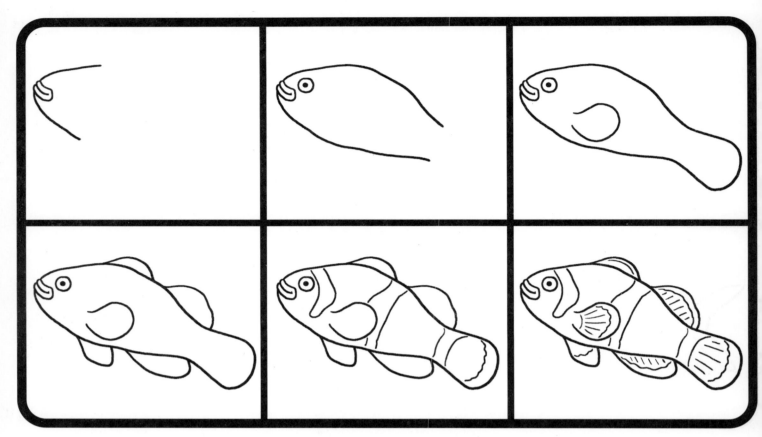

Hammerhead Shark

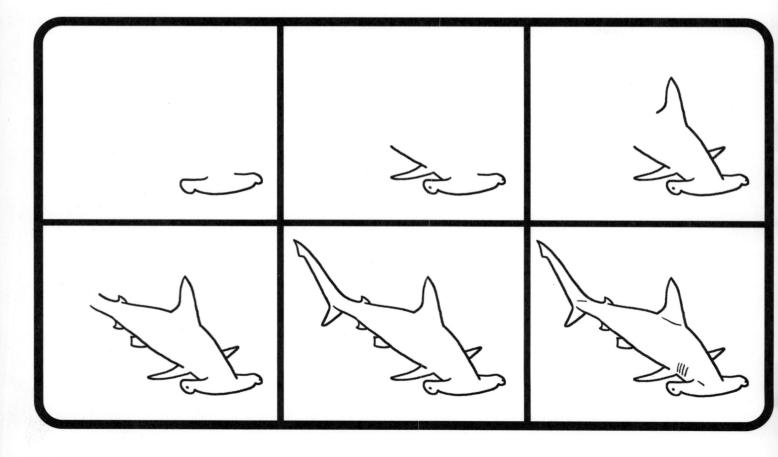

Permit fish

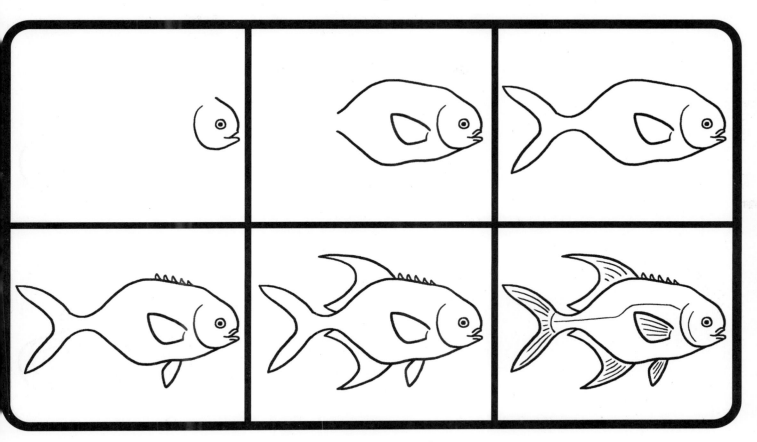

Spotted Dolphin

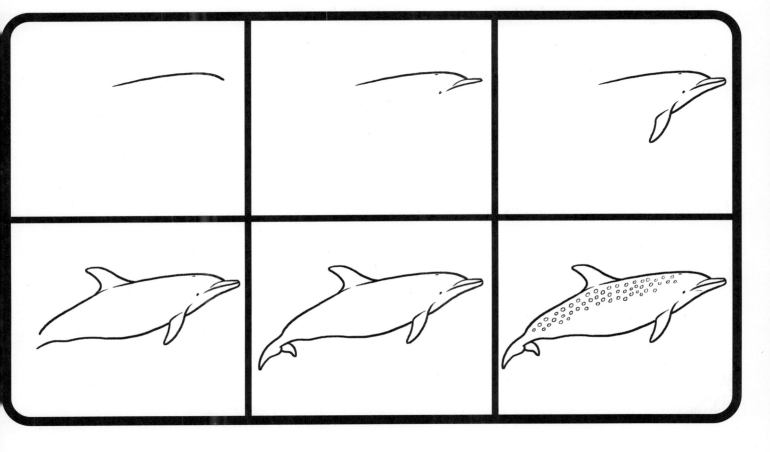

cuttlefish

Pilot Whale

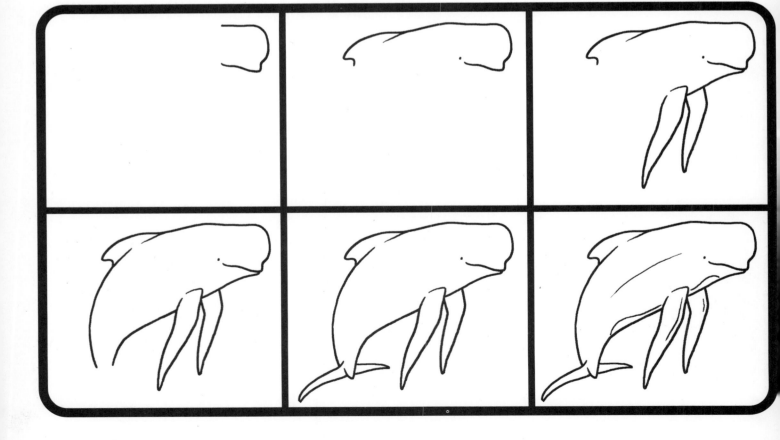

Skate

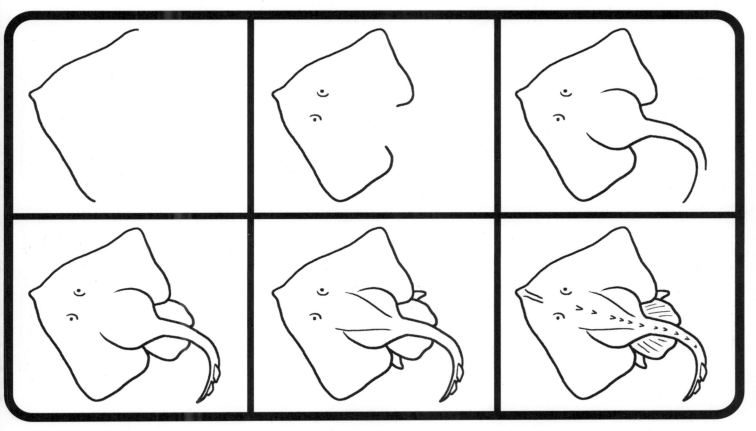

Hermit crab

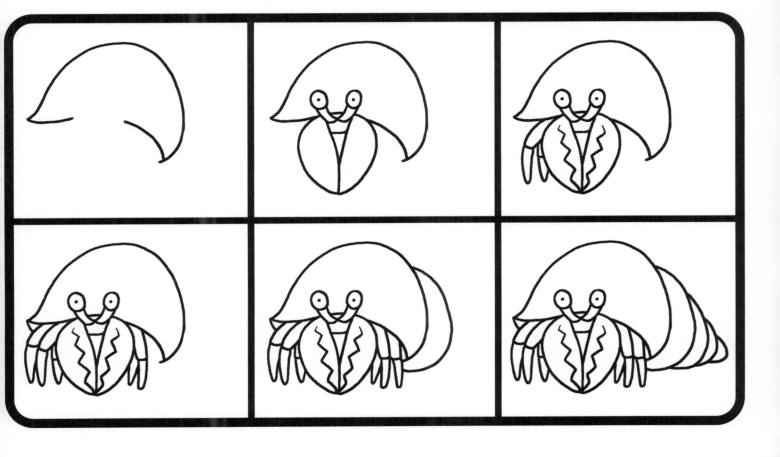

Blue Whale

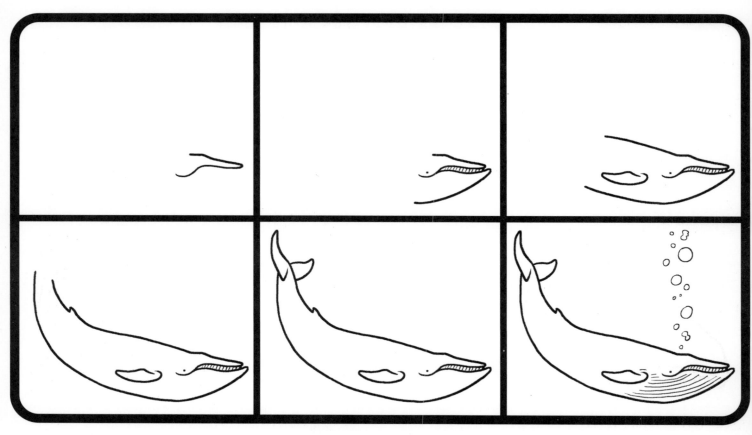

Fire Goby

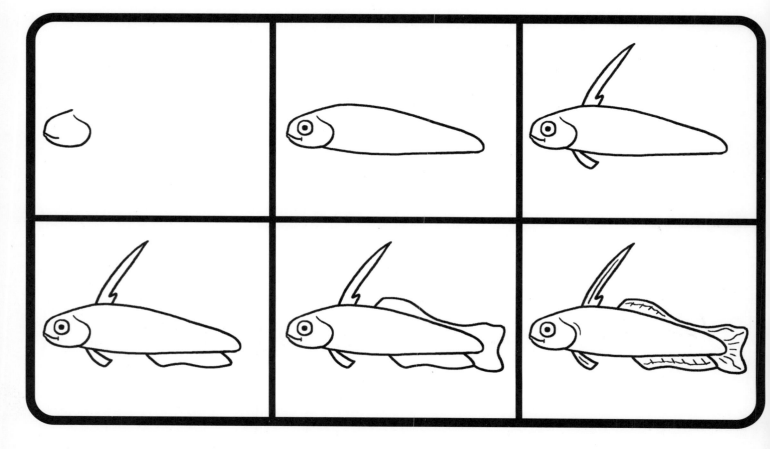

Walrus

Humpback Dolphin

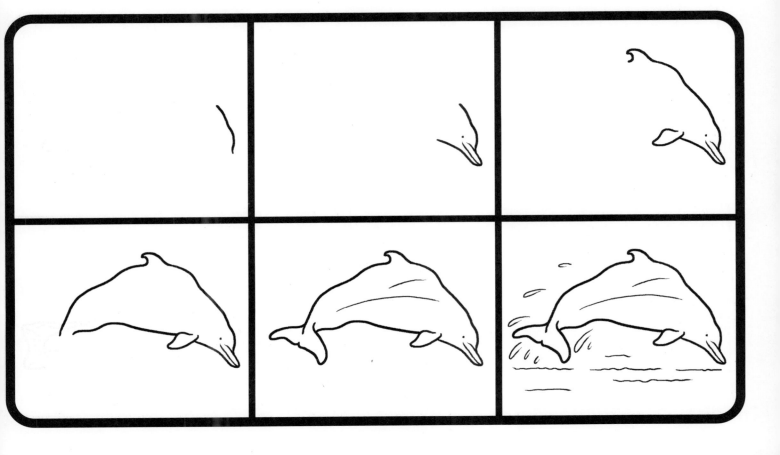

Black Dragonfish

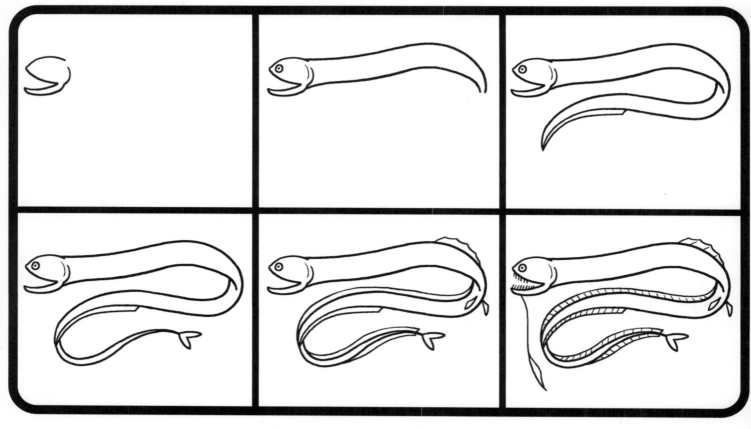

Basking Shark

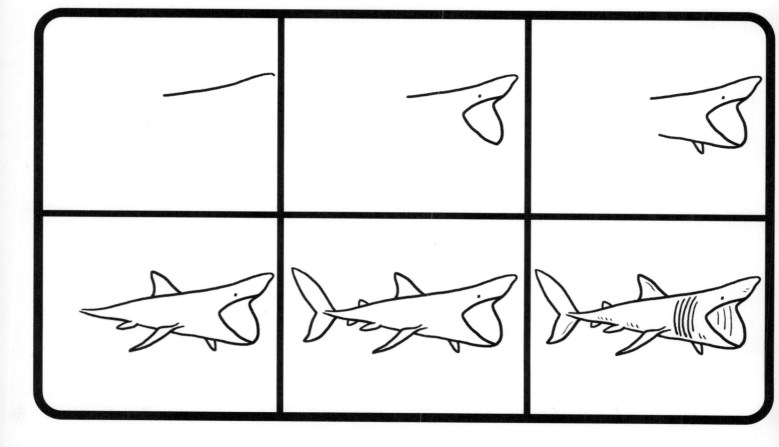

Queen Angelfish

Nautilus

Seagull

Dolphin with ball

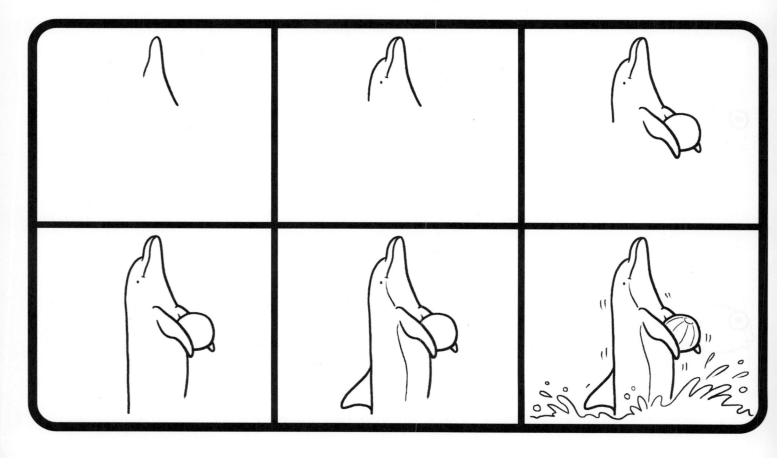

Blue Tang

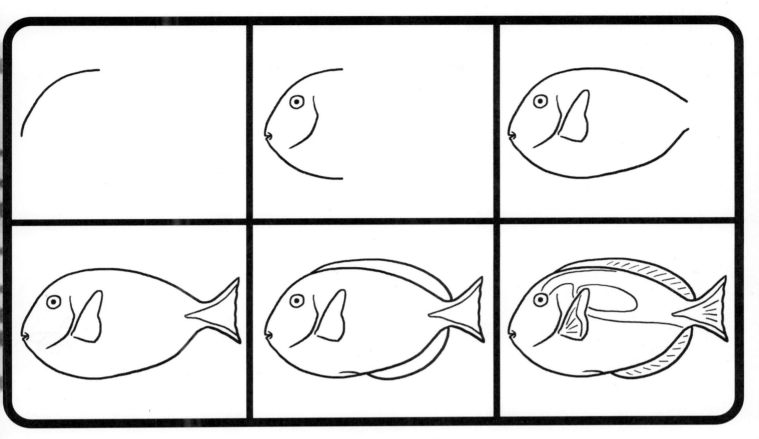

Mandarin Fish

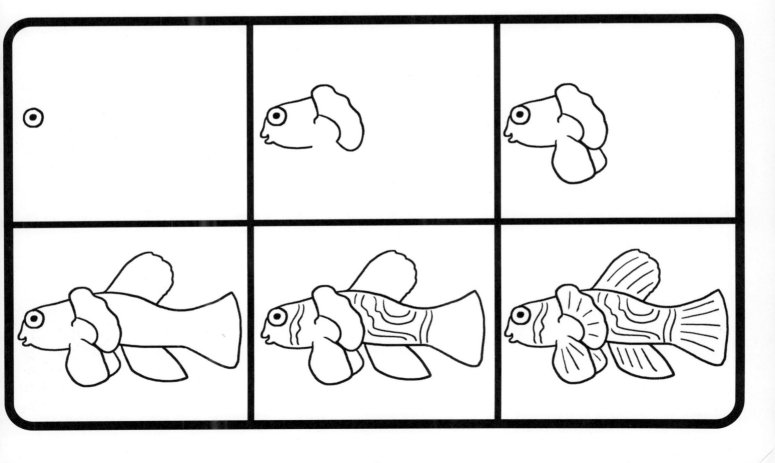

Picasso Triggerfish

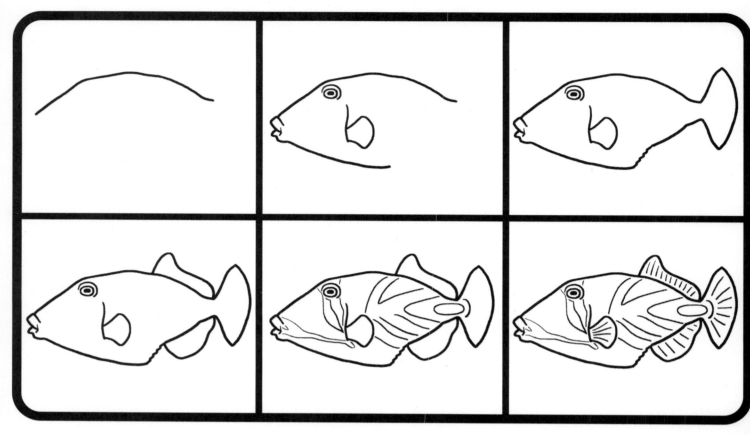

Red Snapper

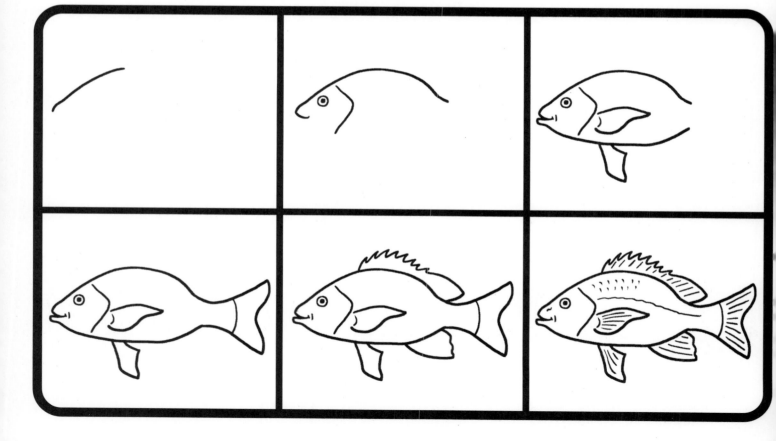

Emperor Penguin with egg

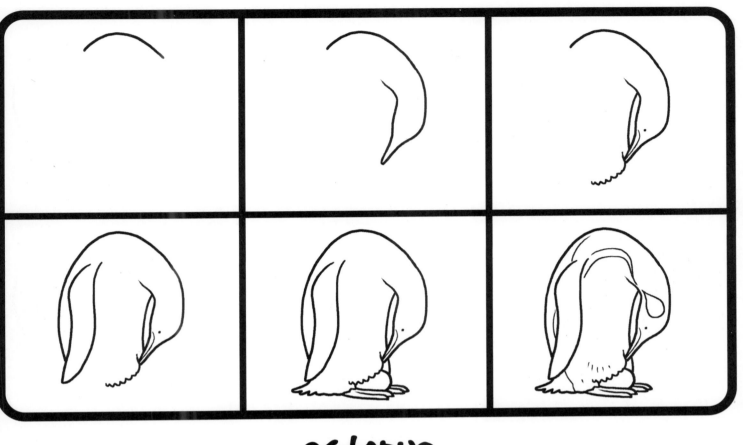

octopus

Dolphin jumping

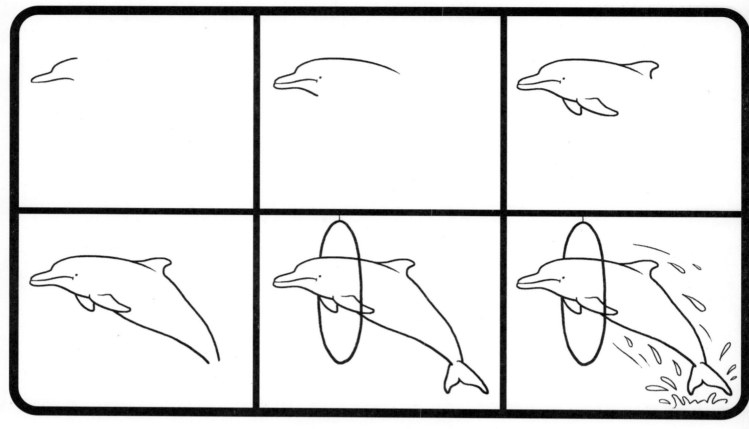

Manta Ray

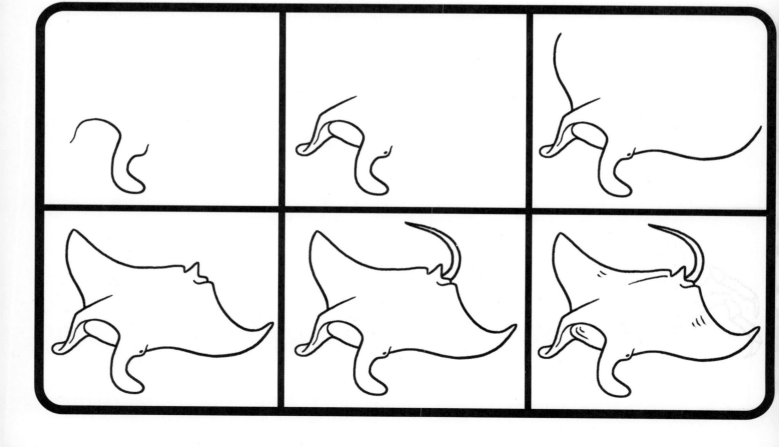

Narwhal

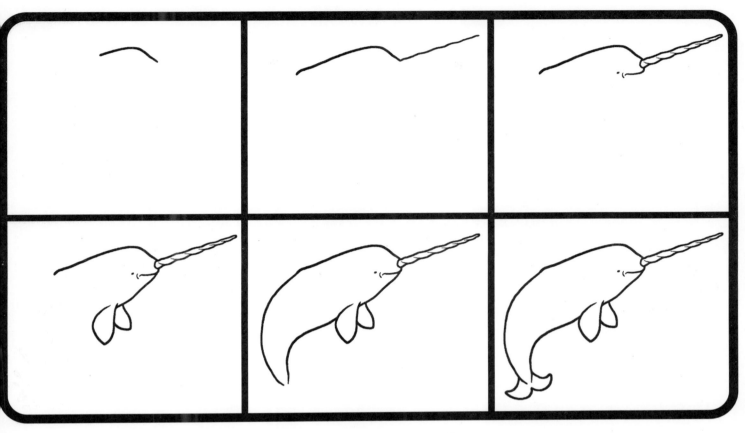

Spider crab

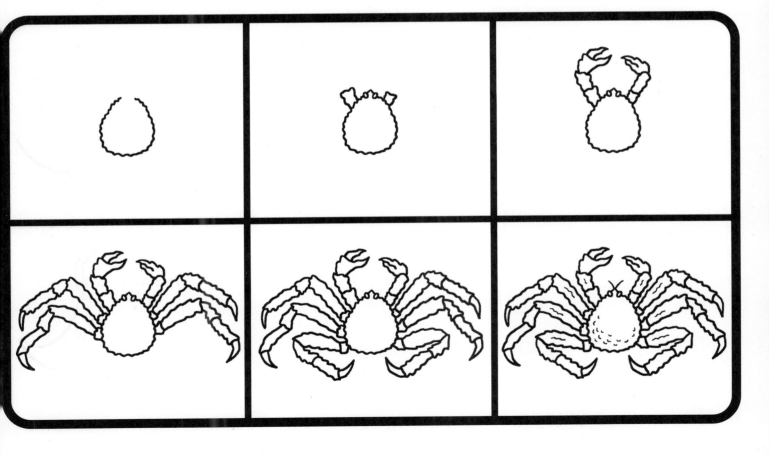

Sea Lion

Soldier Fish

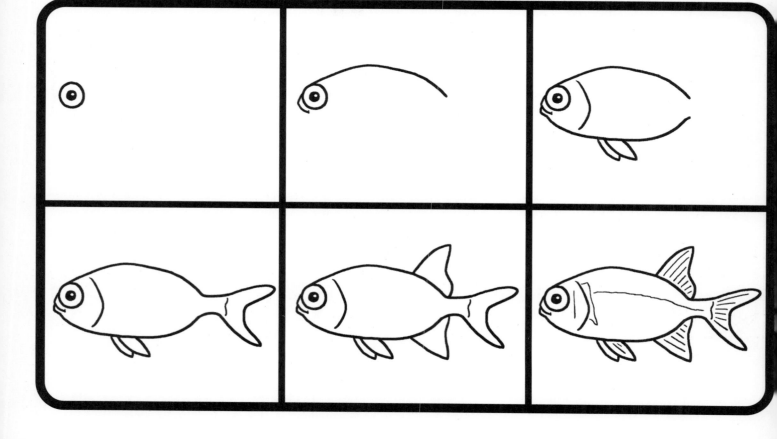

chromis fish

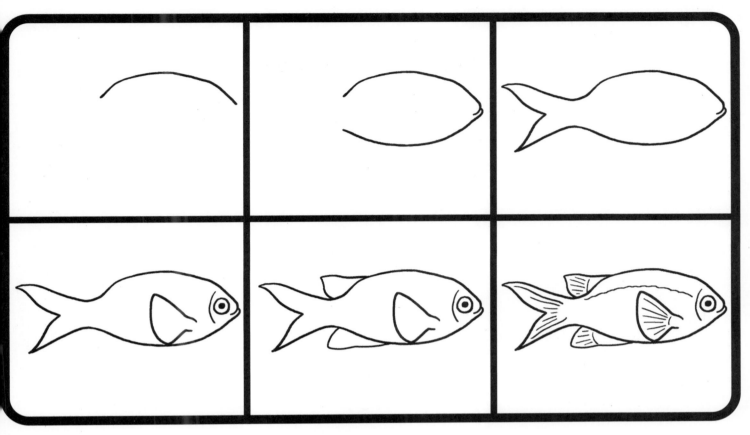

Stingray

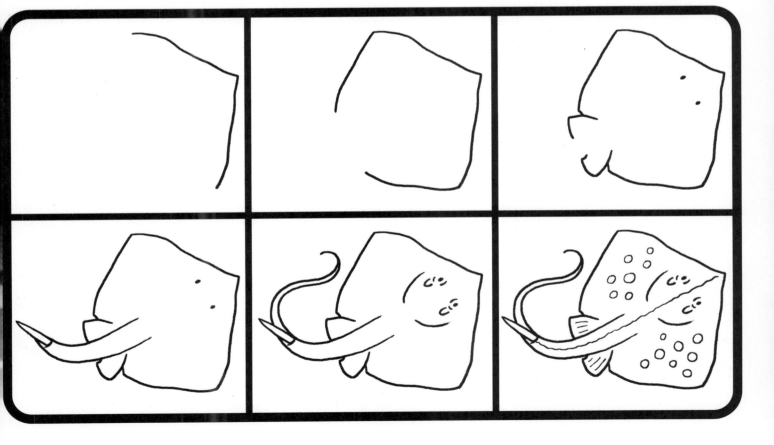

Four-Eyed Butterfly fish

Baby Seal

Dusky Dolphin

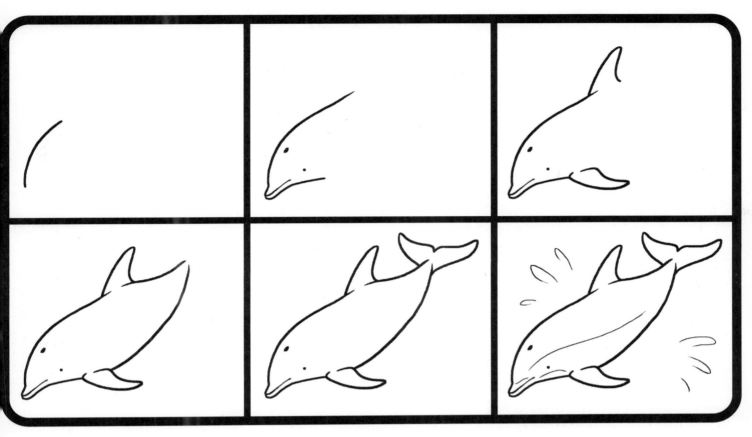

Moonfish

Anglerfish

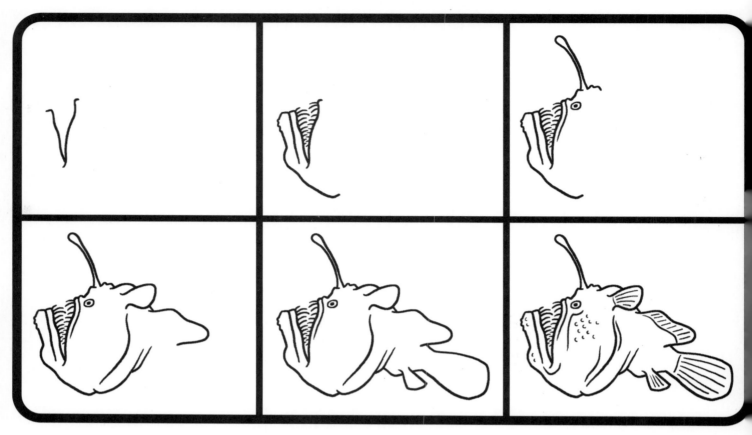

Marine Iguana

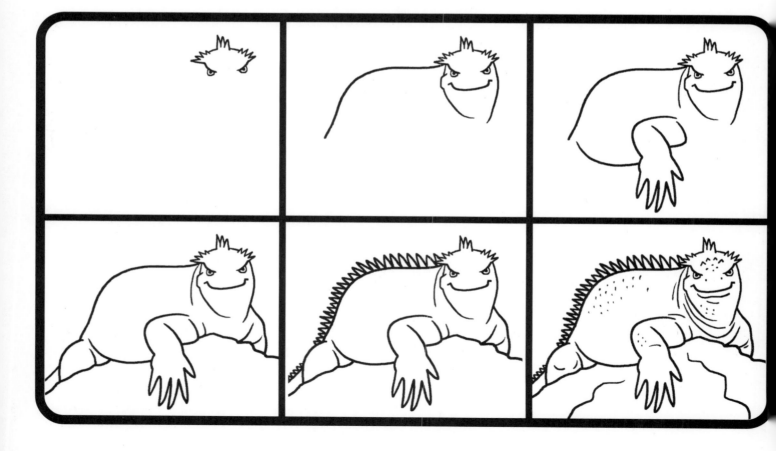

Humpback Whale

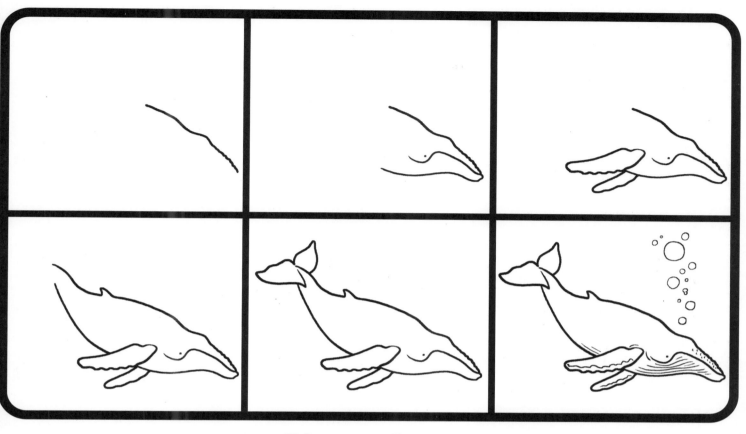

Flying Fish

Elephant Seal

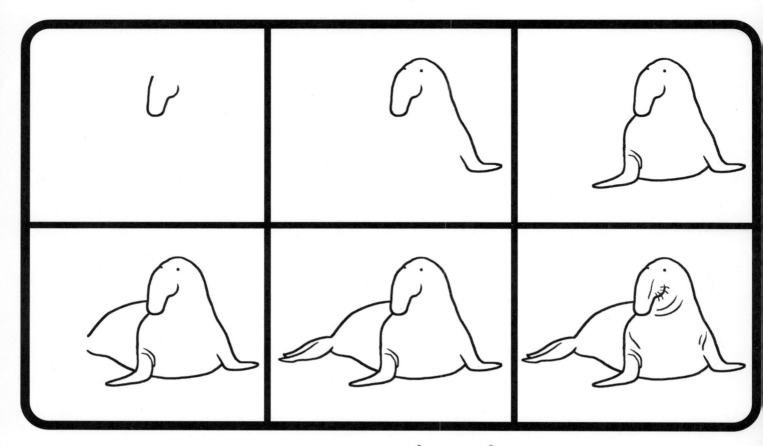

Commerson's Dolphin

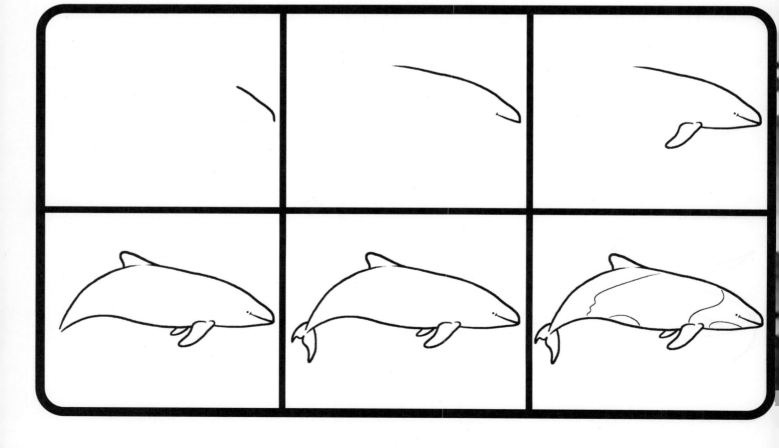

Butterfly fish

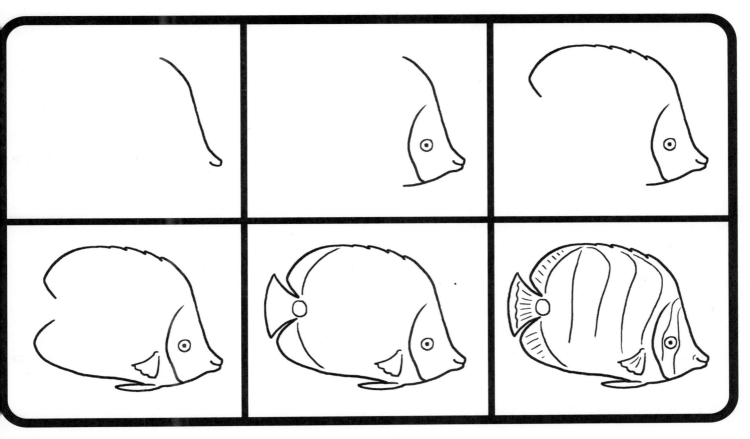

oarfish

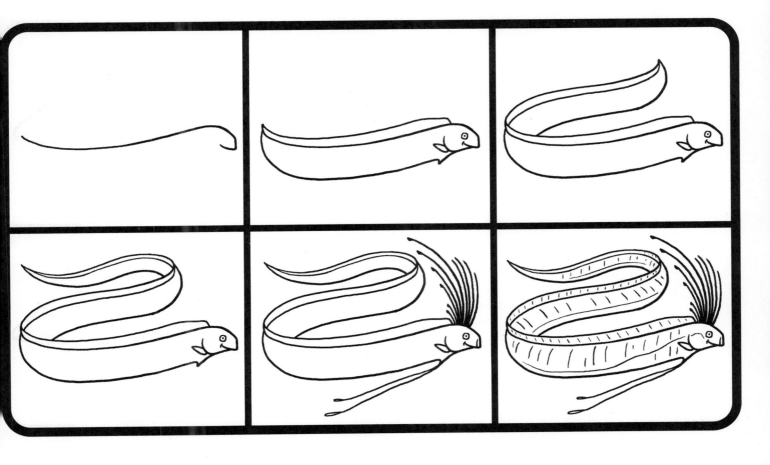

Manatee

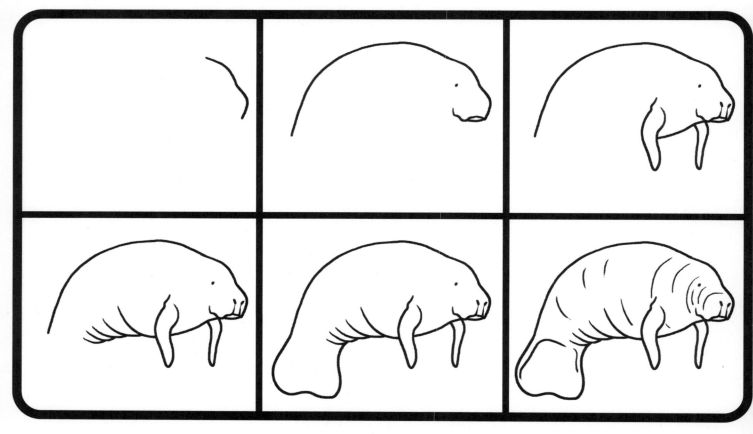

Sea Turtle

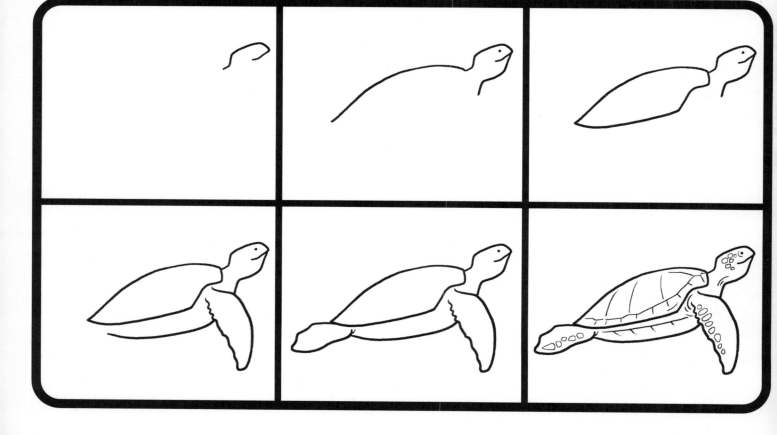

killer Whale (orca)

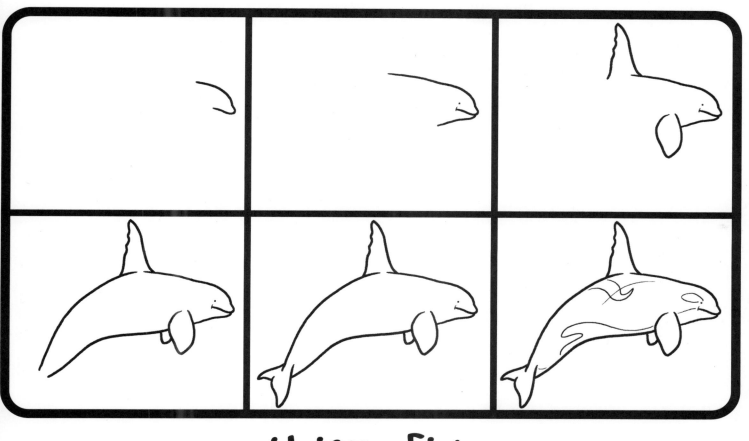

Unicorn Fish

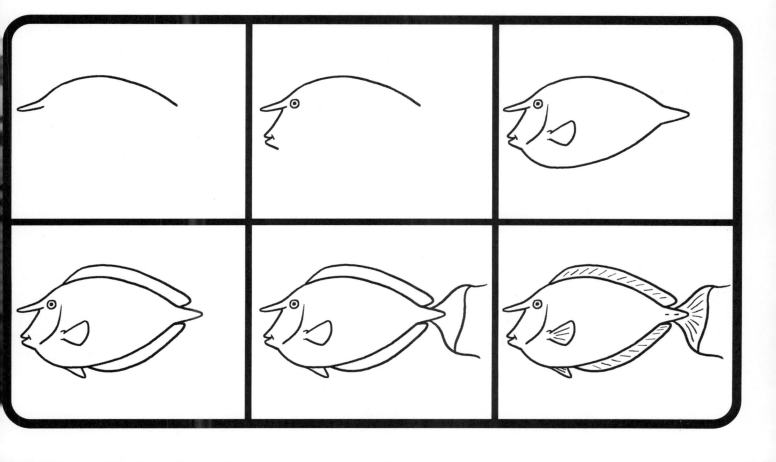

Sailfish

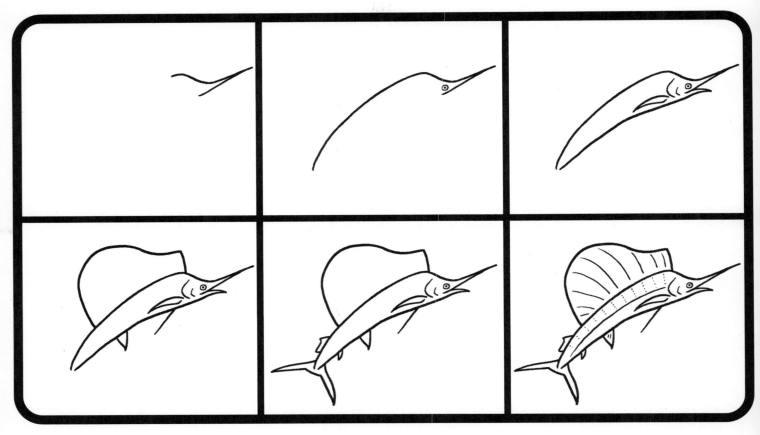

Lumpsucker

Baby Dolphin

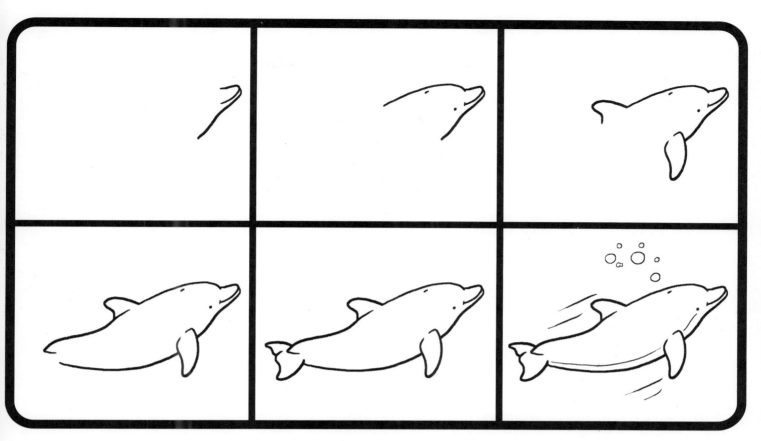

Pineapple Fish

Spotted oreo

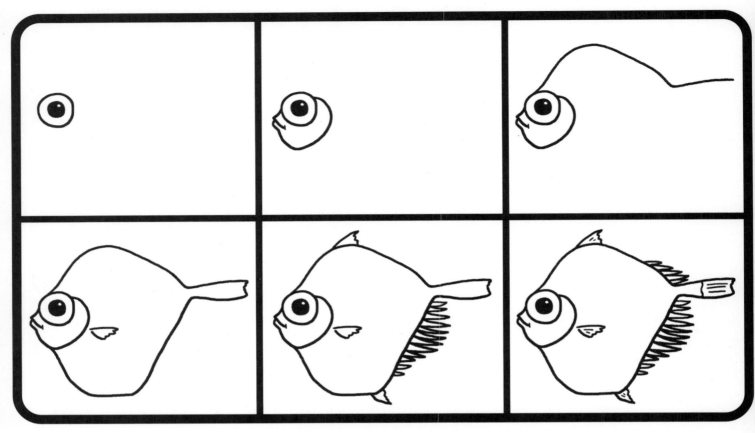

Softshell Turtle

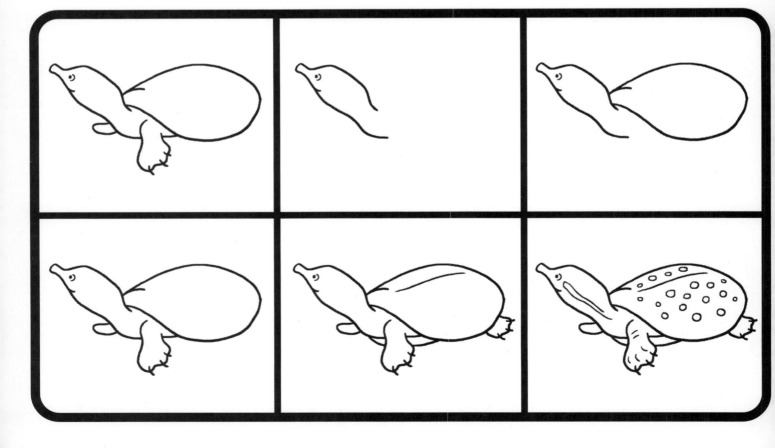

Swordfish

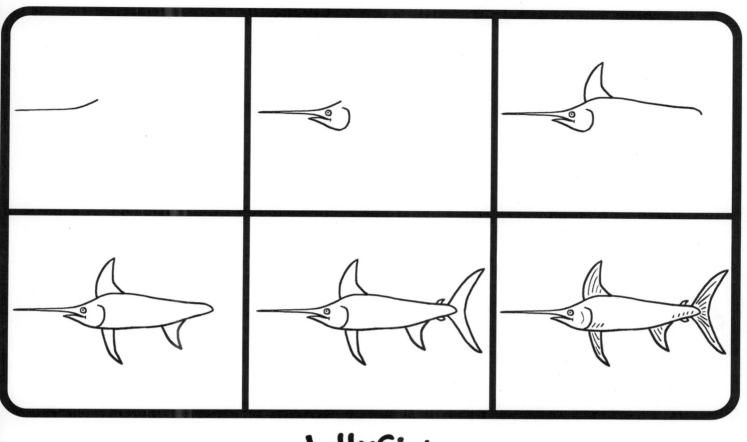

Jellyfish

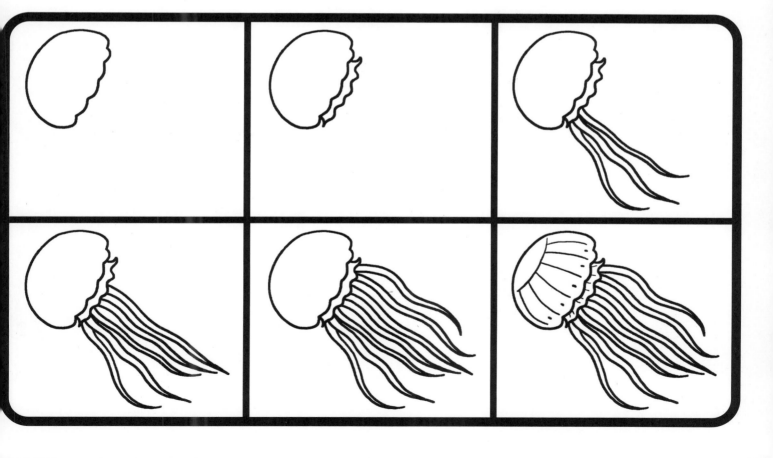

Sea Lion

Blue-footed Booby

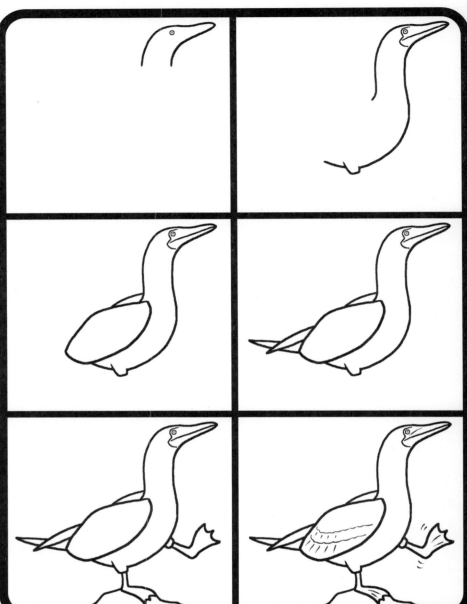

Starfish

Toadfish

cockatoo fish

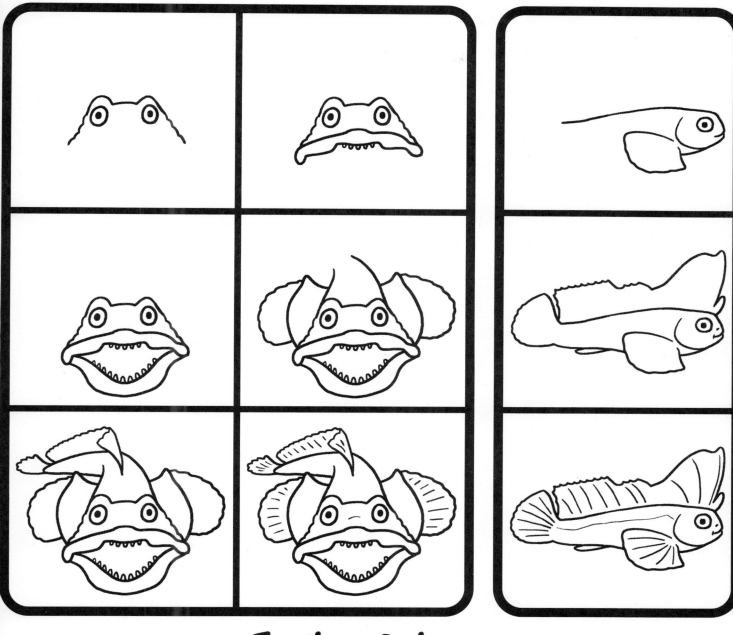

Smiling Dolphin

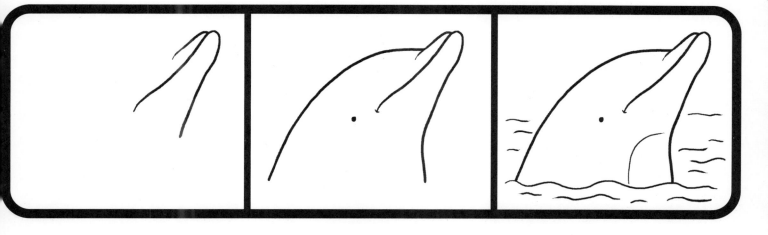

Sea Slug

Sea Otter

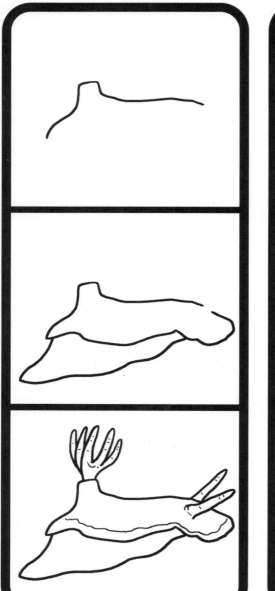

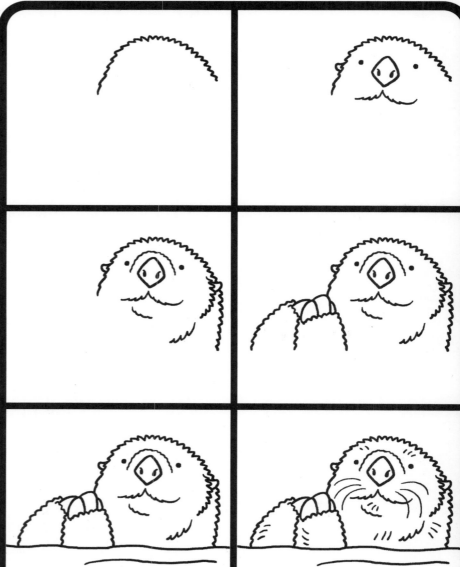

Horseshoe Crab

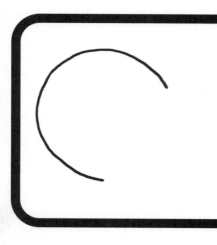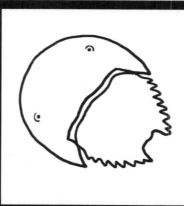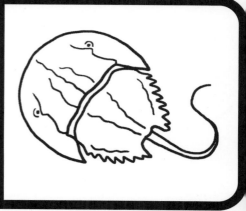

Clown Knife Fish

Moon Jellyfish

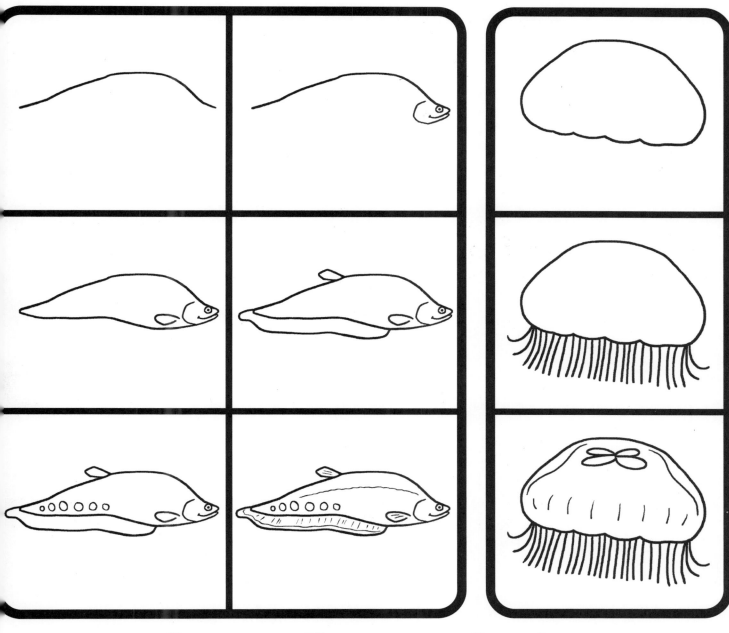

Big-Eye Thresher Shark

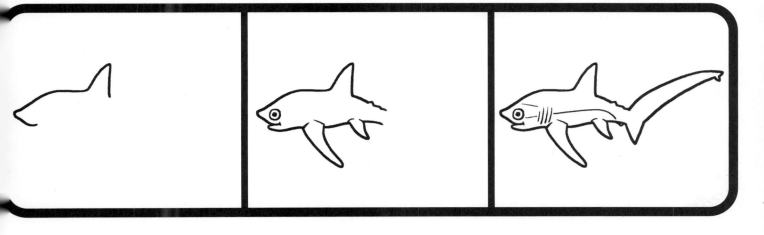

Brittle Star

Tail-Walking Dolphin

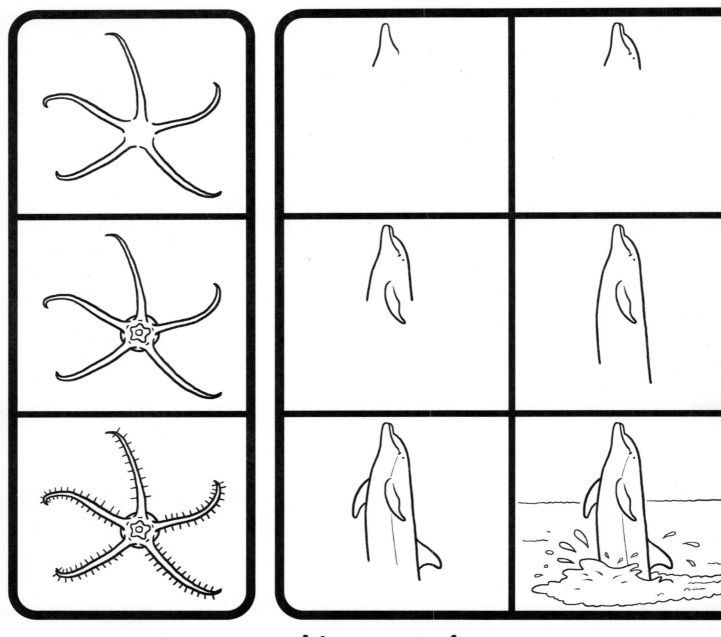

Moray Eel

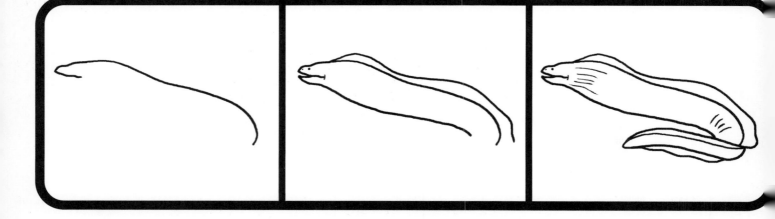